Family Snapshot as a Poem in Time

poems by

G. H. Mosson

Finishing Line Press
Georgetown, Kentucky

Family Snapshot as a
Poem in Time

Copyright © 2019 by G. H. Mosson
ISBN 978-1-63534-849-1 First Edition
All rights reserved under International and Pan-American Copyright Conventions. No part of this book may be reproduced in any manner whatsoever without written permission from the publisher, except in the case of brief quotations embodied in critical articles and reviews.

ACKNOWLEDGMENTS

To Arabella & Atlas, for your gifts of being. Of your earliest years, which you're outgrowing, these poems humbly honor.

To Dave Smith, Amanda Greene, Meryl Peters, and Marcus Colasurdo, for your support and encouragement, thank you.

Publisher: Leah Maines
Editor: Christen Kincaid
Cover Art: Atlas Mosson, "Wow" (2018)
Back Cover Art: Arabella Mosson, from "Landscape" (2018)
Author Photo: Patricia Bennett
Cover Design: Leah Huete

Printed in the USA on acid-free paper.
Order online: www.finishinglinepress.com
also available on amazon.com

Author inquiries and mail orders:
Finishing Line Press
P. O. Box 1626
Georgetown, Kentucky 40324
U. S. A.

Table of Contents

Family Snapshot as a Poem in Time

I	1
III	2
V	3
VII	4
IX	5
X	6
XI	7
XII	8
XIV	9
XVI	10
XVIII	11
XXI	12
Remarks: By The Window	13
XXIV	14
XXVII	15
XXVIII	16
XXIX	17

Peek-a-Boo Moon and Other Poems

Hello Moon	20
Let Us Count the Stars	21
Snuggle Song	22
Sleepy Dance	23
Peek-a-Boo Moon	24
Prayer for the Moon	25
Dawn Moon	26
Chasing the Moon	27
Afternoon Moon	28
Good Morning Sunrise	29

FAMILY SNAPSHOT AS A POEM IN TIME

I.

. . . .When did the beginning dive within

and when did my past become ▮▮▮▮▮▮▮▮▮▮▮▮

Let me fall down on my knees and pray to you—O invisible—

▮▮▮▮▮▮▮▮▮▮▮▮▮▮▮▮▮▮

▮▮▮▮▮▮▮▮▮▮ I run from the busy roads

where it is comic to walk on our brother's back, cross

our sister's throat just to drink a glass of water before noon.

I guard my windows. ▮▮▮▮▮▮ Let me be quiet

as a mouse in a hole, and watch winter's frost perspire off

slick black branches. ▮▮▮▮ ▮▮▮▮▮▮▮▮

▮▮▮▮▮▮▮▮▮▮▮▮▮▮▮▮

Yet ▮ Spring will come. ▮▮▮▮▮▮ I too am young.

I wish I had thoughts equal to Spring.

Notes for Development: Leave as is. No, I can't.

III.

▮ supposed to be writing this everyday—but life got in the way, like it usually does, ravenous—I don't even know when I ▮ arrived back ▮—▮ writing ▮ mirror—and ▮ decided to date everything, pin it ▮ down, just like now on Feb. 22, 2013▮ ▮ ▮ If I steer ▮ carefully, will I end up in safe harbor? That's not all I ask. ▮ I want ▮ what's wonderful for my children▮ ▮ silence behind ▮ eyelids when I sleep ▮ ▮ pre-dawn ▮ with coffee and ▮ books to stretch out forever, ▮ yet, ▮ also for my sleepy daughter to droop into the living room ▮ into my hug. Soon my son toddles out. I wake ▮ my wife and go to work. ▮ ▮ Not much has changed ▮ ▮ ▮ For I still want it all.

Remarks: Dear mirror, always with me.

Notes for Development: Make this a snapshot. . . .

V.

 stumbled against a tree ▮▮▮ and glanced behind to see ▮▮▮

▮▮▮ a newborn ▮ a body ▮ now ▮▮▮ dressed in ▮▮▮ this shared living ▮▮▮

and the sun rises ▮▮▮ larger than ▮▮▮ our creations ▮▮▮
What did I come here to say ▮▮▮
by a tree ▮▮▮ ▮▮▮

▮▮▮ father of two ▮ 38 ▮▮▮ writing about how I got here ▮▮▮ becoming ▮▮▮

Remarks: I remain grateful for Spring.

Notes for Development: Focus. . . .

VII.

▬▬▬▬▬▬▬▬▬▬▬▬▬▬▬
▬▬▬▬▬▬▬▬▬▬▬▬▬▬▬▬▬
▬▬▬▬▬▬▬▬▬▬▬▬▬▬▬▬▬▬
▬▬▬▬▬▬▬▬▬▬▬▬▬▬▬

▬▬▬▬▬▬▬ Firecracker daughter, ▬▬▬▬▬▬
your volcano of energy exhausts my imagination. I always thought
imagination meant walking in a moonlit field weeping ▬▬▬▬▬
▬▬▬▬▬▬▬▬▬▬▬▬▬▬▬▬▬▬
▬▬▬▬▬▬▬▬▬▬▬▬▬▬▬▬▬▬▬
▬▬▬▬▬▬▬▬▬▬▬▬▬▬▬▬▬▬
▬▬▬▬▬▬▬▬▬▬▬▬▬

Where was I? And where have I traveled to? The easy answer: time.
▬▬▬▬▬▬▬▬▬▬▬▬▬▬▬▬▬
▬▬▬▬▬▬▬▬▬▬ And ▬ though my imagination soars
in ▬▬ wee hour▬▬▬▬▬▬▬ through sounder grooves
than ▬▬ younger days, it cannot outrace you
▬▬▬▬ daughter▬▬▬▬▬▬▬▬▬▬▬▬▬ as I laugh,
or break, ▬▬▬ from lack of knowing
▬▬▬▬▬▬▬▬▬▬▬

Song: From hunger, cycle . . . from churning, our song. . . .

Notes for Development: Leave it raw? Is less, more?

IX.

███████████████

███████████████████

█████████████████

███ a symphony ██ captures the hindsight

██████████████ as I walk you in the stroller

and you and your brother point ██████ at the moon?

There is no symphony██████████████

to encase our evening, between dinner and bath,

████████████████████

████████████████

████ as ██ day falls through deep seams █████

██████ through ██████ ranges of ████████ *aaaaaaaaaa* ███████████ night.

Remarks: I wish I knew.

Notes for Development: Cut, cut, cut.

X.

So this is mid-life: a ▮ window ▮▮▮▮

▮▮▮▮▮▮▮▮▮▮▮▮▮▮▮▮▮▮▮▮ kaleidoscope

▮▮▮▮▮▮▮ embroidered scarf ▮▮▮▮ picture

in a shoebox ▮▮▮▮▮▮▮▮▮▮▮▮▮▮▮▮▮▮

▮▮▮▮▮▮▮▮▮▮▮▮▮▮▮▮▮▮▮▮

▮▮▮▮▮▮▮▮▮▮▮▮▮▮▮▮ groceries

▮▮ mouthwash for myself, ▮▮▮ toothpaste for my daughter,

a toothbrush for my son to maw and look up at me, grinning copyist.

▮▮▮▮▮▮▮▮▮▮▮▮▮▮ I glance back:

▮ some distant person running, happy, stupid, and ▮▮▮▮

▮▮▮▮ my kids tumble in squeals ▮▮▮ onto the porch.

My son points up into the tall▮ sky with whistling birds that criss-cross

the pre-spring. The moon. He points and utters and smiles.

▮▮▮▮▮▮▮▮▮▮▮▮▮▮▮▮▮▮▮▮

▮▮▮▮▮▮▮▮▮▮▮▮▮▮▮▮▮▮

The moon, I say ▮ and point. He grins and nods

and knows the word and points again. Yes, the moon.

Song: When I was young, how I shook the night of its apple.
           When I was young, how I awaited the amphitheater of stars.
           Tonight, my kids sleep on the other side of the porch wall. My wife paints.
           Do they know this dreamer? They must, for they come from our dreams.

XI.

███████████████████████████
███████████████████████████████
████████████████████████████████████
██
██
████████████████████████████████████ March 21, 2013

I stand on the ledge of ████
████████ swaying blackened trees,
██
██ son ██ daughter ██ asleep █████████ wife ██████ emerged █████,
then ███ back to bed. I sit in my chair. I have nothing to say or reflect
████████████████████████████████
from which I could launch myself. ███████████████████
██
█████████████████████████████████████ Now is where I stand
█████████████████ through action ██ words █████████████ intent.
██████████████████████ I intend to love.

Song: Sing, muse, of fatherly love, of
parents yearning like ships; sing of
motherly love, of union that births
forth living joyful answers; how late
or soon, quick wits turn back with questions.

Notes for Development: Allow room. Use a close-up.

XII.

Reading a stray comment, almost graffiti, about Antler's poem *Factory*,
██
"what's going on in the world" and ████████████████████
felt free again to think ███████████ ████████████████
████████████████████████████ felt, again, we live to do more than just live.
Why not say it█████████████████████████████████
even if ████████████████████████████████
███ so few walk naked in the streets to call our attention to the righteous life.

████████████ American poets ████████████████
██ mimic ██████████████████████████
car, house, █ adultery, █ paycheck████████████ kid's soccer game;
so what ███████████████████████ they keep telling;
so what this plainspeaking, █████████████ so what this aspiration;
so what this inspiration, so what this striving █████████████
██████████████████████████████████████, ███
follow the righteous path and there █████████ be who you are.

Remarks: Emerson's "American Scholar," Whitman's "Poem of Nakedness," Antler's *Factory*, Ben Franklin's *Autobiography*, Adrienne Rich's "Atlas of a Difficult World," Martin Luther King's challenge, Gandhi's walk. . . .

Notes on Development: Hands off.

XIV.

████████████████████████████████
████████████████████████████████████
██
██
██
██
██████████████████████████████████
████████████████████████████████████
█████████

Will you get smaller?	asked my daughter.
Yes, I'll seem less taller	when you get older.
Then I'll carry you? She smiled.	When bigger, I replied.
And go to work in your black car	*and use your black computer?*
Dad, you'll stay home?	Yes, alone.
Though maybe you'll stop by?	*No*, she didn't lie.
When you're not busy?	*Okay maybe.*

██
██████████████████████████████████████
████████████████████████████████████
██████████████████████████████
████████████████████████████████

Remarks: Loosen the lens.

Song: Tonight I never want to let you go.

XVI.

How do you put together a marriage

over the ▆▆ road of years? How ▆▆▆ look down that road

and see yourself at the end, planted, rooted, sun-filled, lazily arrived?

▆▆▆▆▆▆▆▆▆▆▆▆▆▆▆▆▆▆▆▆▆▆▆▆▆▆▆▆▆▆▆▆

▆▆▆▆▆▆▆▆▆▆▆▆▆▆▆▆▆▆▆▆▆▆▆▆▆▆▆▆▆▆▆▆

▆▆▆▆▆▆▆▆▆▆▆▆▆▆▆▆▆▆▆▆▆▆▆▆

▆▆▆▆▆▆▆▆▆▆▆▆▆▆ I wish I was an arrow. I wish I could move

faster than my mind. I wish I was that river flowing furious ▆▆ not too far ▆▆▆▆▆▆.

XVIII.

First I had a vision, then I had a life.

The daffodils came with spring. Did they ever sing?

The winter was a time to hone. I am no longer alone.

Did the summer stretch out endlessly? Did the fall entangle me?

Two years ago I showed my daughter the moon. I am too tired for stars.

Yesterday, my son watched a squirrel climb a utility pole. His eyes bulged.

I took him down the slide for the first time, in spring's first glorious afternoon.

His mind rearranged. He stomped to the playground steps with a wild surmise.

For me, what's amazing has changed.

XXI.

After the rainbow, choosing the path;

After the fury and passion led you into a partner, choosing the partner;

After the meadow and its flowers owned your soul, choosing the Sunday walk there;

After all the tears and the joys, it's a quiet Sunday, only, and choosing to swim in the quiet;

sail here now upon the silence and see, out of the corner of your eye, the other strollers, silent also, and now all slogans and banners, the Victorian chairs and postmodern sunglasses, fall off like rain from clouds, and the clouds are transparent; the transparency is nakedness that no clothes shelter nor hide. I walk my soul today. I walk on the wall's serrated top. I dance on each of its edges. I look afar and close. Rain falls. I become soaked. I grow alive, feel hate, feel love. Time rolls beneath my fingers like counting beads. I count them. They add up to this: Choose wisely.

Remarks: By the window with spring arriving again, I see broad green-blues of twilight enter our home. In the kitchen, my daughter and son chirp about my wife, who's patching together dinner, well rested and happy to have painted during her free time today, while I lurked about, somewhat sick, off from work, cooked, cleaned, and took the kids to the park. Old jeans and favorite sweater buffered me in near-frigid April weather. Let the wolves howl and the vultures feast elsewhere. We too shall fight, but not right now.

Song: Lullaby me, roofless night,

> *With your cat feet clocks and dark tree tips,*
>
> *Whisper through this core your soundless space, until*
>
> *I'm swallowed into these drops of listening.*
>
> *Even as night's invite prods hunger, with*
>
> *Time's anvil waiting for the next ringing dawn, don't*
>
> *Let me pass into the gridded human world*
>
> *Without your subtle touch.*

Notes of Development: Hectic indoor days. Must get organized. Where was I? Okay, a long poem. It's going to be about my life. How can I write it without editing my life into what I wish? How can I write this life, as is, from the point of view of the writer's mind? How embarrassing. There must be some sort of useful blindness, delicious dizziness that blurs into wholeness, carving out an internal vacuum of calm core from the errata. Okay, don't change a word. But don't show them all. Use black-out. Less is more. To catch the dance that comes and goes, to capture feeling foremost without the used furniture of facts, yet not vacationing in the ideal lounges of memory, this art must steer perspective through practiced forgetting, as if some dancer launches from posture into grace.

XXIV.

If I am not a dreamer, how will my son know me?

▮▮▮▮▮▮▮▮▮▮▮▮▮▮▮▮▮▮▮▮

These days I walk ▮▮▮ between ▮▮▮▮▮

▮▮▮▮▮ older self, gaze ▮▮▮▮▮

▮ April moon ▮▮▮▮▮ blue daylight

▮▮▮▮▮▮▮ daughter ▮▮▮▮

▮▮▮▮▮▮ day's close ▮▮▮▮

▮▮▮▮▮ change ▮▮▮▮ how it hides.

Tonight my shoulders are heavy with work's haul.

▮▮▮▮▮▮▮▮▮▮▮▮▮▮▮▮

Yet I owe more thanks than I can summon.

Song: Beneath a sky of wishes, / the afternoon's shawl / in the lost and found / and so I put it on. / Did it adorn my charcoal suit / like your arms did once? Well—shouldered
        it forward. Got stuff
        done. Wore it
        home. Never
        returned that luck-
        y omen, amused
        vagabond that I am
        who's vigilant still
        for such tossed
        off talismans
        discarded past any-
        one's claiming.

Notes of Development: More song.

XXVII.

Dear Daughter, you may read this, long after I've ceased

reading you to sleep, and just memories sing for us the old lullabies.

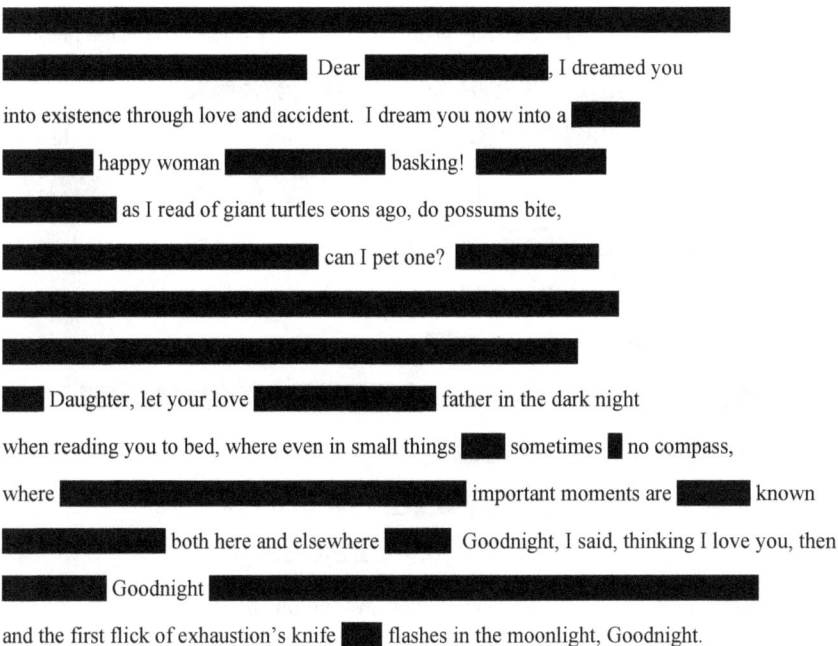

███ Daughter, let your love ███████████ father in the dark night

when reading you to bed, where even in small things ███ sometimes █ no compass,

where ███████████████████████ important moments are ██████ known

████████ both here and elsewhere ████ Goodnight, I said, thinking I love you, then

████████ Goodnight ███████████████████████████████

and the first flick of exhaustion's knife ███ flashes in the moonlight, Goodnight.

Remarks: Let this be a message in a bottle. I have mailed it to myself and one day I'll open it. If I throw it in the ocean, what songs circle back first? Will I hear myself or hear it as someone who knows them? I'll probably look away if the weathered bottle washes back into my hands. Overwhelmed by the erasing cradle of waves, who is to say this score is mine? Okay, song, I own you, because I can face you tonight.

XXVIII.

Dear Son, our morning together stays with me
this Saturday night in the library at work on duties and dreams. Tonight's tasks:
Walt Whitman and bankruptcy, a May poem and editing an article on pension law.

███████████████████████████████████████

███████████████████████████ As Rumi said, these words ██ are fallen leaves
compared to looking into your eyes ████████ ██████████████████
████████████████████████ that even when I seek peace, and hear your dawn cry
and bleary-eyed patter from bed, I pick you up, and hold again.
We've read together many mornings ████ with your mom and sister asleep.
You ██████ listened even to the poems ██████████████████████████
████████████████████████████████. What you recall
of me, my son ██████████████████ escapes my hands
as quickly as it will escape yours. Yet you will stand, having drunk
of my essence and of your family and of your own burning heart.

████████████████████████████
████████████████████
████████████████████████████████
████████████████████████████████

XXIX.

████████████████████████████████

████████████████████████████████

what glasses of tears will make us smile,

what rains of joy will make us one day shiver?

████████████████████████████████████
████████████████████████████████████
██████████████████████████████
████████████████████████████████████

Notes of Development: Moonlit new clouds.
                                                Close up at night.
                                                Among shadows.

Remarks: Turning to the past for refuge.
                                                Turning ahead with hope.
                                                Turning to the mirror with wonder,
                                                then back to the flow.

Song: Spring awaits us.
                                                Colors are mute teachers.
                                                Tears are just one experience of flowers.

PEEK-A-BOO MOON & OTHER POEMS

HELLO MOON

Thinnest crescent in the night, your moonbeams gleam
a tinsel light, and two tiny stars nearby
are just as bright.
   I think you'll play
      together tonight
         when I'm not watching.

From my bed, through this window, I send you a smile
for you're just three sharp sparks
in the black wild.
   I must sleep soon
      cocooned in my room.
         Hello moon, goodnight.

LET US COUNT THE STARS

Let us count the stars.
Show me where they are.
One, two, three . . .
my Daddy says to me.

Silver brightness lights
the vastness of the night
where the moon is never fixed.
Four, five, six. . . .

Let us count the stars.
Point to where they are.
How far my fingers roam . . .
before returning home.

SNUGGLE SONG

When the house is hush
and the games put away
and my mess of milk
cleaned up with the day,
and the baby in bed,
soon Mom and Dad too,
and the windows tremble
with rain passing through;
and the house is too hush
and the games far away
and I'm stuck where I'm tucked
in a bed where I wait
while the milk in the fridge
calls out through the dark
and my brushed teeth
can't change what I want,
so I cry and then wail,
and Dad comes to me.
He reads me a tale
which I know, so I sleep.
Yet the wind still whispers
and again I'm awake
and now Mom is here
to hush my tears
and takes me with her
to sleep in their bed,
and feeling such rest
snug in their nest,
I fall fast into
sleep's hand,
dream's land.

SLEEPY DANCE

In the darkest hush, with both eyes shut, yet still
      I cannot sleep. My Daddy comes and picks me up—
           it's where I want to be.

In night's hug, as violet fog
      swirls between the trees, I grin as Daddy walks the porch.
           I'm where I want to be.

I glimpse how snakes of silver mist
      ripple toward our feet—yet high above, like a nested bird,
           I'm where I want to be.

On shoulder mountain, in alpine arms,
      Dad's pacing cradles me, yet I'm falling, falling
           like finest rain to where I want to be.

PEEK-A-BOO MOON

Where is that moon, as night soars overhead
just speckled with stars? Did the moon go to bed?
Do you dance with the sun? Do you play with the sea?
Does the moon swim with dreams to help hope be free?
My Dad brought me out, and Mom came too.
Peek-a-boo Moon, where are you?

PRAYER FOR THE MOON

As afternoon darkens, the closest trees dim
and a first star sparkles. Sky's blue thins
and shadows spread.
      Hurry up, Moon!

As we stroll, we're watched, for I hear an owl call.
The street is vacant, not one leaf falls.
No squirrel jumps.
      Hurry up, Moon.

The next star appears above the dusk's blush.
Hoot-hoot zigzags across the hush.
There's home, let's rush.
      Come on, Moon!

As sunset thins and falters, falters
and fades, as twilight fades and zeros,
      Moon, lantern my way.

DAWN MOON

Half-Moon in blue,
why are you
awake too?

Lunar head,
the horizon's red,
so go to bed.

Bone-white and swelled,
with magic spells,
I won't tell.

Here comes Sun,
Yellow Lion.
You'd better run!

Unearthly bloom
on time's loom,
see you soon.

Good day, Half-Moon,
I hope that you
liked my tune.

CHASING THE MOON

In the tangle of trees,
    a hazy golden moon
        hammocks in a cave
            within a smoky glow.

A few clouds cross. Stars blink hello.

Through gold lagoons
    where cloudlets bronze and laze
        in dusk's perfume,
            you sneak and hide. We seek!

AFTERNOON MOON

This afternoon, the moon
        mammoth among the sky
above the tree line looms
        a marbled gray-and-white.
And why did you come so soon
        so mute in the blue of the sky?
I still see, as if in childhood,
        how you married day and night.

GOOD MORNING SUNRISE

Good morning, golden red,
how quick you let me see:
first the trees in silhouette,
then the trees in green.

From the East, expanding rays
see-saw the stars away,
then within slip and thin
the darkness into day.

I'm awake! I'm awake! tweets a bird
from inside the green weave of a tree,
as I peek out the window to see
while sunrise tickles the sleepy.

G. H. Mosson is the author of three prior books of poetry, *Heart X-rays* (PM Press, 2018, with Marcus Colasurdo), *Questions of Fire* (Plain View, 2009), and *Season of Flowers and Dust* (Goose River, 2007). His poetry and literary criticism have appeared in *Measure, Tampa Review, Cincinnati Review, Smartish Pace,* and *Rattle*, among other journals, and his poetry has been nominated four times for the Pushcart Prize. He also edited the anthology, *Poems Against War: Bending Towards Justice* (Wasteland Press, 2010). He holds an MA in writing from the Johns Hopkins Writing Seminars, and BA in English. Mr. Mosson is a father, writer, lawyer, and dreamer. He practices employee rights and disability rights law as well as civil litigation. He hails from NYC and lives in his second home-state of Maryland.

www.ingramcontent.com/pod-product-compliance
Lightning Source LLC
LaVergne TN
LVHW041506070426
835507LV00012B/1370